Frankenstein

and Other Stories of Man-made Monsters

Eric Kudalis

Capstone Press

MINNEAPOLIS

Printed in the United States of America.

Capstone Press • 2440 Fernbrook Lane • Minneapolis, MN 55447

Editorial Director   John Coughlan
Managing Editor   John Martin
Copy Editor   Theresa Early
Editorial Assistant   Michelle Wood

Library of Congress Cataloging-in-Publication Data
Kudalis, Eric, 1960-
    Frankenstein and other stories of man-made monsters /
Eric Kudalis.
        p. cm. -- (Classic monster stories)
    Includes bibliographical references and index.
    Summary: Dr. Frankenstein creates a monster, which escapes and comes to an unhappy end. Includes information about the original story, different movie versions, and the scientific aspects behind the story.
    ISBN 1-56065-213-6 (lib. bdg.)
    [1. Monsters--Fiction. 2. Monsters.] I. Title. II. Series.
PZ7.K94855Fr 1994
[Fic]--dc20   93-42831
                                               CIP
                                               AC

ISBN: 1-56065-213-6
99 98 97 96 95   8 7 6 5 4 3

Table of Contents

Chapter 1

Frankenstein

There are many stories of man-made monsters. The best known of these is the story of Dr. Frankenstein and his monster. Even though Frankenstein is the name of the scientist, most people refer to the monster itself as Frankenstein.

The story of this monster first appeared in a book in 1818, and since then many versions have been told in plays and movies. Most people know the story from the **classic** 1931 movie, *Frankenstein*.

The Story of Dr. Frankenstein

Dark clouds hovered above the cemetery as

mourners gathered around an open grave. A priest said a prayer over the coffin.

Dr. Henry Frankenstein and his hunchbacked assistant, Fritz, hid behind tombstones. They waited patiently.

Finally the priest led the mourners away through the dark. The grave digger threw the last scoop of dirt onto the grave.

"Yes! Now we can get the body and begin our experiment," Frankenstein said.

They crept toward the grave. Fritz began digging. Faster and faster he dug until he hit the coffin.

"Quick, pull up the coffin," Frankenstein commanded.

Frankenstein jumped into the grave to help Fritz. As he lifted the coffin, Frankenstein held it close to him.

"He is not dead," Frankenstein said. "He is only resting, waiting for me to give him new life."

A Stolen Corpse

Frankenstein and Fritz stuffed the body into a large sack and dragged it out of the cemetery. They headed toward Frankenstein's laboratory.

On the way, they saw a body hanging from a **gallows**.

"Cut him down," Frankenstein said. "We need his brain."

Fritz hesitated, then he cut down the corpse. The body hit the ground with a thump. Frankenstein grabbed it.

"The spine is broken. The brain is no good. We'll need to get another brain."

Frankenstein looked at Fritz. "You must go to the medical school tonight and steal a brain."

An Abnormal Brain

Fritz set out for the medical school. He hid outside an open window until the last student left the building. Then he crawled through the window and scurried toward a science table. On the table were two brains in separate jars.

One jar was marked "normal brain." The

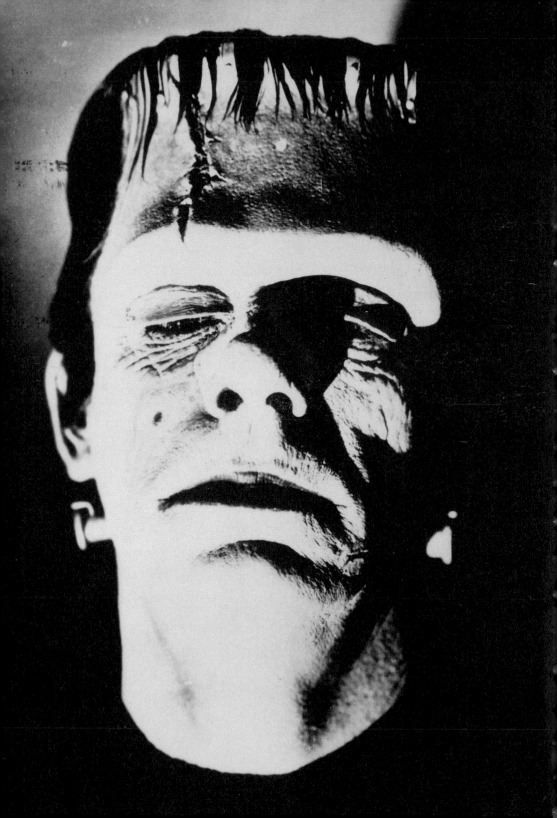

other was marked "**abnormal** brain." But Fritz couldn't read.

He snatched the normal brain. Then he heard a noise in the hallway and jumped. He dropped the jar. The brain splattered across the floor. Frightened, Fritz grabbed the other jar and ran back to his master's laboratory.

Frankenstein's Obsession

At Castle Frankenstein, Henry's **fiancée**, Elizabeth, paced back and forth. She was worried about Henry's strange behavior. Victor, Henry's best friend, tried to comfort her.

They decided to go see Professor Waldman, Henry Frankenstein's former teacher.

In his office on the medical-school campus, Dr. Waldman talked to Victor and Elizabeth. He said that Henry Frankenstein had become **obsessed with** creating life. Frankenstein wanted to play God, Waldman said. He wanted to breathe new life into dead human bodies.

The three of them decided to go to the

watchtower of Castle Frankenstein. There Henry made his strange experiments.

As they left, a gust of wind surprised them. A storm was approaching. Lightning lit up the sky.

In Frankenstein's Laboratory

The watchtower stood high on a hill. The old stone walls were cracked and crumbling. Inside, the rooms were dark and musty.

Henry Frankenstein was hard at work in his laboratory. Heavy machines hummed with energy.

A stretcher stood in the center of the lab. It was attached to steel cables and a pulley. On the stretcher lay a body covered by a sheet.

Frankenstein turned to Fritz. He had to shout because the storm was becoming louder and louder.

"There's no blood. Only stitches holding the different body parts together."

Frankenstein pulled the sheet away from the head.

"The brain is inside him now," he said. "In a body that I made from the corpses we stole."

The body needed only one thing now. A jolt of electricity from the lightning would give it life.

Frankenstein's Experiment

Frankenstein and Fritz were ready to raise the body toward the roof. Thunder was pounding. The noise was deafening. But it was more than the thunder and lightning. Someone was at the door. Pounding. Screaming.

"Let us in! Henry, let us in! We need to see you!"

Fritz ran to the front door. "Go away!"

Elizabeth called out, "Henry, it's me."

Frankenstein motioned for Fritz to open the door.

"So you've come after me, have you?" he said. "You think I'm mad, don't you? My experiment will prove that you're mad for not believing me."

He told them that he had experimented with animals and that he was ready for his greatest experiment ever–to give life to a human being.

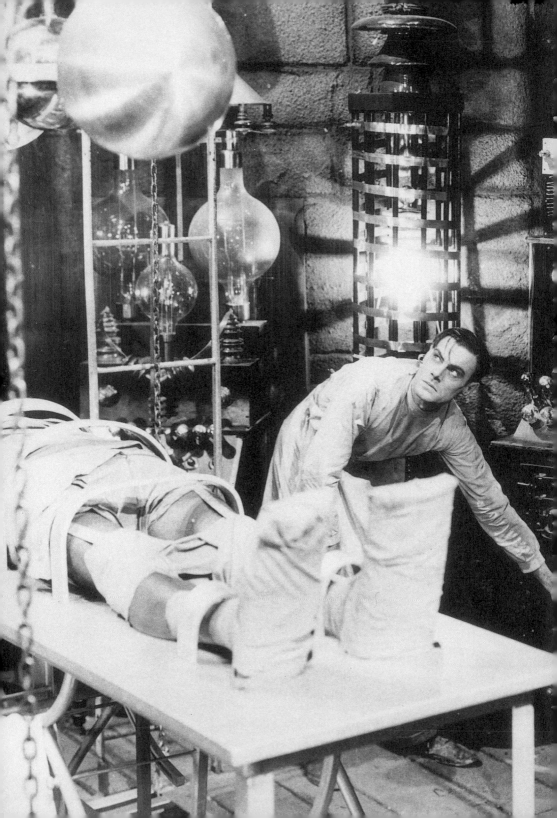

"It's Alive!"

"Follow me," Frankenstein said.

Fritz tugged at the pulley. The stretcher with the body rose up through the tower, toward the sky.

Elizabeth, Victor, and Dr. Waldman watched in disbelief. Lightning struck the stretcher. The room lit up.

Fritz lowered the stretcher.

Frankenstein waited eagerly.

A hand hung from the side of the stretcher. First a finger moved. Then the entire hand. Finally the arm raised itself.

"It's alive. It's alive!" Henry screamed. "I've created life."

The Brain of a Murderer

The next day Henry Frankenstein bragged about his success. Dr. Waldman was not so pleased.

"No good will come of this. This monster you created will destroy you. That brain Fritz stole was the brain of a murderer."

They heard footsteps in the next room and

turned. The creature was standing in the doorway.

He was tall and had dark, sunken eyes. His shoulders were broad. The creature looked frightened and confused. He seemed unsure of his steps.

Suddenly the creature is alive!

Henry Frankenstein called out. "Come here. Sit down."

The creature walked slowly toward him and sat in a chair.

"You're Frightening Him!"

Fritz was jealous. Frankenstein saw only his creature. Fritz didn't like the creature.

Fritz teases the creature with a burning torch.

Fritz picked up a burning torch and began **tormenting** the creature.

"Stop that! You're frightening him!" Henry yelled.

Henry and Dr. Waldman managed to calm the creature. They chained him in a dark room and left him alone.

But Fritz sneaked into the room that night and teased him with a torch.

The creature broke loose from the chains and grabbed him.

The Creature Can Kill

Henry and Dr. Waldman heard a horrible scream. They rushed to the creature's room. Fritz was dangling from a hook.

The creature moaned and grunted. He looked at the two men and **lurched** toward them. He grabbed Henry Frankenstein and shook him.

Dr. Waldman stabbed the creature with a needle filled with a drug. The creature tumbled to the floor.

"Now do you believe me when I say no good

will come of this?" Dr. Waldman asked Henry. "Go away with Elizabeth and I will kill the creature."

The Creature Kills Again

Henry went to his father's home at Castle Frankenstein to recover. He and Elizabeth began to make wedding plans.

Dr. Waldman was getting ready to experiment on the creature.

The creature woke and grabbed the professor. Dr. Waldman struggled, but he was too weak. He fell to his death. The creature ran from the laboratory and into the countryside.

Outside Castle Frankenstein, the villagers prepared for Henry and Elizabeth's wedding.

In the countryside, a girl named Maria was playing by a lake. She looked up and saw the creature standing over her.

"Who are you?" Maria asked. "Do you want to play with me?"

She led the creature to the water's edge and handed him several daisies.

At first, Maria does not understand how dangerous the creature can be.

She threw a daisy into the water. Then he threw a daisy in the water.

"See, they float," Maria said.

The creature smiled at her.

Maria threw another daisy in, then he threw another in. Soon there were no more daisies left.

The creature reached for Maria. He picked her up and tossed her in the water like a daisy. Maria screamed, but no one was there to help her.

"I Have Created a Monster"

Back in the village, the townspeople danced in the streets. Inside Castle Frankenstein, Elizabeth prepared for her wedding. She could not escape her fear, though.

Victor rushed into the castle. He called out, "Dr. Waldman is dead! The creature killed him. Now it is loose in the countryside."

Henry Frankenstein was horrified. He locked Elizabeth in her room so the creature could not get to her.

"I have created a monster!" he cried. "We must find him and kill him before he does more harm."

They heard a moan. They knew the creature was inside the building.

"Let's search the castle. He's in here somewhere," Henry said.

He and Victor searched everywhere but could not find the monster.

A Close Call

Elizabeth sat alone in her room. She felt something **hovering** above her. She looked up and saw the creature.

He looked deep into her eyes. Then the creature came toward her.

Elizabeth screamed. All the wedding guests ran to Elizabeth's room. By the time they got there, the monster was gone.

To Kill the Monster

In the streets, people were singing and dancing. They were celebrating the wedding.

They stopped when they saw a woodsman stumble through the street. He was holding the lifeless body of his daughter Maria.

He went to the mayor's house.

Elizabeth shrieks as the monster comes toward her.

"My daughter is dead. She's been drowned. Murdered," the man said.

"The monster did this," the villagers called out. "We must destroy it."

Frankenstein heard about the murder. He joined with the crowd.

"I made the creature with my hands," he said, "and now I will kill it with these hands."

Frankenstein Found the Monster

The villagers formed a large mob. With torches in hand, they headed to the woods. They would find the monster.

Henry Frankenstein ran ahead of the crowd. As he stepped from behind a boulder, he saw the creature. They stood still, staring at each other.

The creature lunged at Frankenstein. He tried to scare it with the torch, but the creature was not afraid.

Frankenstein screamed. The monster smacked him to the ground. Before the mob could come to the rescue, the creature dragged Frankenstein off.

The End of Frankenstein's Monster

Frankenstein awoke in an abandoned windmill. He felt weak. He stumbled up from the floor.

The monster grunted. He grabbed Frankenstein and threw him against the balcony. The crowd gathered at the base of the windmill.

The monster hurled Frankenstein over the balcony.

Frankenstein was knocked out by the fall. But he was still alive.

The crowd began to shout, "Burn the mill. Burn the monster."

They set their torches to the windmill. Flames quickly climbed up the walls and jumped to the roof.

The creature was frantic. He dashed from one side of the mill to the other. There was no escape. The mill collapsed in flames. The monster screamed as he burned.

Dr. Henry Frankenstein's evil experiment finally was ended.

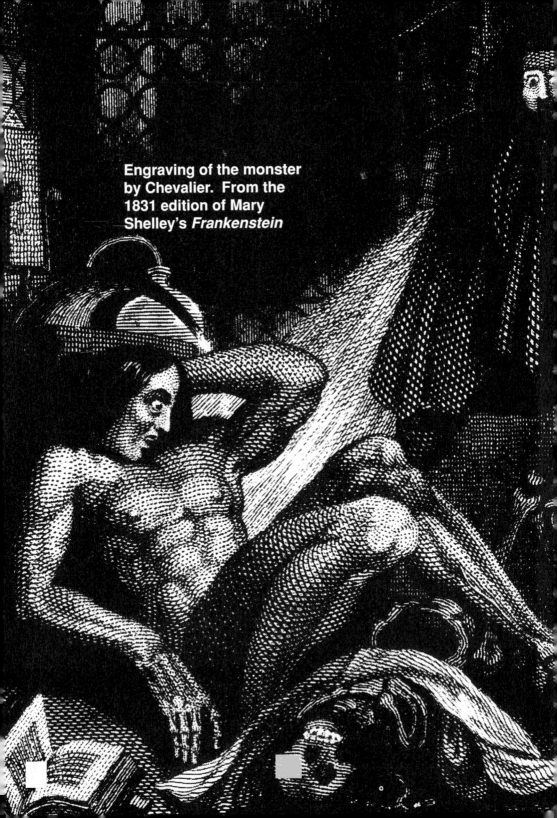

Engraving of the monster by Chevalier. From the 1831 edition of Mary Shelley's *Frankenstein*

Chapter 2
Mary Shelley

*F*rankenstein, produced by Universal Studios in 1931, is one of the most popular horror films ever made.

The film of Frankenstein's monster is based on a book by the English author Mary Wollstonecraft Shelley. She lived from 1797 to 1851.

The Story Behind Frankenstein

Mary Shelley's novel, *Frankenstein*, was published in 1818.

Mary Shelley wrote the book while vacationing in Switzerland. She was with her future husband, the English poet Percy Bysshe Shelley, and several friends.

One night the friends challenged one another to write ghost stories. Mary's tale became the book *Frankenstein*.

The Original Story of Frankenstein

The book is different in many ways from the story told in the 1931 movie. In the book, for instance, Frankenstein's first name is Victor, not Henry.

The novel is written as a series of letters explorer Robert Walton writes to his sister. Walton tells how he rescued Victor Frankenstein from a drifting iceberg. Frankenstein told Walton his story.

Frankenstein had been born in Switzerland. He had learned the secret of life. He had even created a living human being.

When Victor realized he had created a monster, he was horrified. He abandoned the monster, and left home to forget it.

Frankenstein learned that his brother had been murdered, so he returned home. On the way, he saw the monster by the shore of a lake.

Frankenstein thought the monster had killed his brother.

Frankenstein was afraid to tell the world about his creature. He remained silent. His loyal servant was **executed** for the crime.

Victor Frankenstein felt terribly guilty. He began a journey. In the French Alps, he saw the creature again. The monster told him how lonely he had been.

The Frankenstein monster is lonely and rejected in many of the monster stories.

Unlike the monster in the 1931 movie, Mary Shelley's creature could speak. He told Frankenstein that loneliness and rejection had made him evil.

In the end, Frankenstein died in the Arctic. The monster left for the North Pole, where he planned to kill himself.

A lobby card from *The House of Frankenstein*, 1944

Chapter 3

Versions of the Frankenstein Story

Many plays and films have been based on the story of Dr. Frankenstein, who wished to create human life. Even though Frankenstein is the name of the doctor, people usually call the monster by that name.

Frankenstein Plays

Mary Shelley's book was published in 1818. Soon after, stage plays were written about Frankenstein and his monster. Many early plays changed the story. It was too hard to recreate all the book's scenes on a stage.

Frankenstein was first staged at the English Opera House in London in 1823. In a French production in 1826, the monster was created by magic and destroyed by a lightning bolt.

Frankenstein on Film

The first film of the story was made in 1910 by inventor Thomas Edison. The film was only 10 minutes long, but audiences liked it. No copies of the film exist today.

In 1915, Ocean Film Corporation in New York made a silent film of *Frankenstein* called *Life Without Soul*.

The Classic Film

In 1931 Universal Studios in Hollywood wanted to produce a horror film. *Dracula*, made earlier that year, had been a great

The inventor and filmmaker, Thomas Edison

success. The movie company chose Mary Shelley's *Frankenstein*.

The story as director James Whale told it in the movie is most well known today. Boris Karloff played the monster and Colin Clive was Dr. Frankenstein.

Frankenstein's Bride

In 1935, Universal Studios released another movie about Frankenstein, *The Bride of Frankenstein*. Many people think it is even better than the 1931 movie. Boris Karloff and Colin Clive starred again, and James Whale directed.

In this movie we learn that the monster did not die in the fire.

Now the monster wants a mate. So Dr. Frankenstein goes back to his laboratory to create a female monster. When the new "bride" sees the monster, however, she screams in horror. Rejected, the monster blows up the laboratory, his bride, and himself.

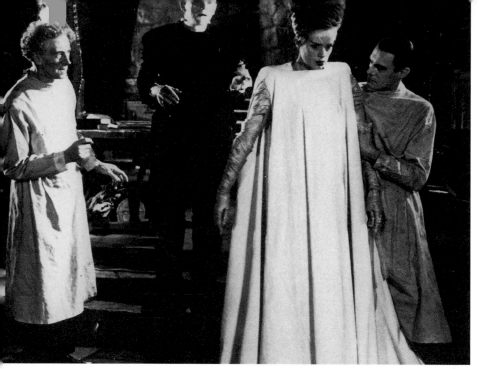

The bride rejects the monster.

Son of Frankenstein

Universal Studios released *Son of Frankenstein* in 1939. Basil Rathbone played Wolfgang Frankenstein, who inherited his father's **estate**.

With his wife and son, Wolfgang travels to Europe from the United States to see his father's **decaying** castle. There he meets Igor, who shows him the body of the monster. Wolfgang sets to work to bring the monster back to life. Boris Karloff played the monster for the last time.

Movies of the 1940s and 1950s

Hollywood produced Frankenstein movies in the 1940s. None were as good as the earlier films.

Abbott and Costello made a comic film in 1948 called *Abbott and Costello Meet Frankenstein.*

In the 1950s, Hammer Studios in England made *The Curse of Frankenstein.* This version was full of blood and gore—all in color.

Peter Cushing played Frankenstein and Christopher Lee played the monster. Hammer Studios made five more Frankenstein movies.

BASIL
RATHBONE
BORIS
KARLOFF
BELA
LUGOSI in

SON of
FRANKENSTE

Lio el AT
JOSEPHIN
HUTCHIN
DONNIE DUNA
Emma Dunn · Edga

Original screenplay by Willis Coo

The character Herman in
"The Munsters"

Frankenstein on Television

The Frankenstein story came to television, too. In 1973, NBC produced a four-hour version called *Frankenstein: The True Story.* It followed Mary Shelley's novel more closely than earlier plays and films had.

But there were still differences in the story. The monster begins as a handsome man. Slowly he becomes uglier and more violent as the movie progresses.

In the 1960s, television audiences enjoyed the series "The Munsters." The character Herman was much different than the earlier Frankenstein monsters. He was fun-loving and harmless.

The scientist Luigi Galvani experimented with electricity and dead bodies. This illustration shows Galvani running electric charges through a pair of frog legs.

Chapter 4

The Science Behind the Story

In the story, Dr. Frankenstein uses electricity to bring his creature to life. When Mary Shelley wrote *Frankenstein*, she based some of her ideas on experiments of the time.

Mary and her friends had discussed the amazing experiments of the Italian scientist Luigi Galvani. They knew that Galvani was trying to see if he could bring dead bodies back to life. In 1803, he sent a high-power electric charge through a human corpse. Witnesses said the dead man actually clenched his fist.

Mary Shelley made this new discovery a part of her story.

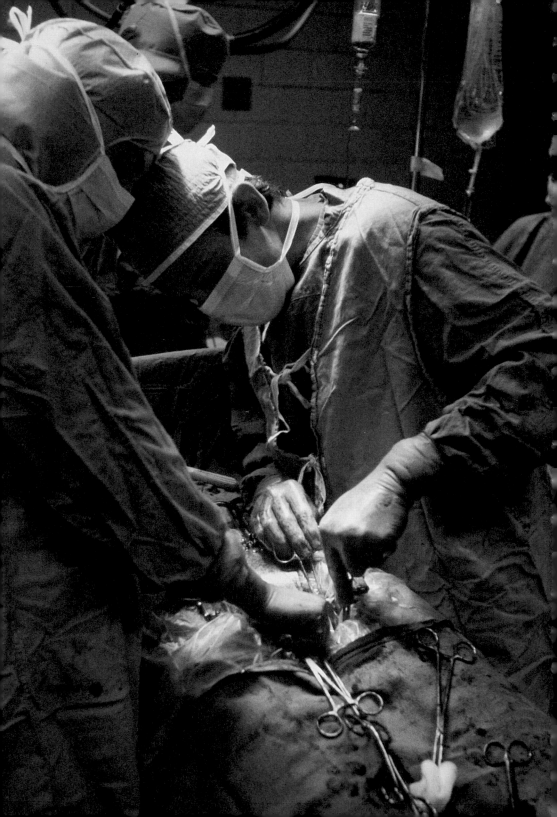

Chapter 5

Organ Transplants Today

Dr. Frankenstein created his monster by sewing together body parts from different corpses. When Mary Shelley wrote *Frankenstein*, this probably seemed like something that could never happen.

Modern Operations

In the 1931 movie, Dr. Frankenstein said that he kept a human heart beating for three weeks. Today, human hearts are commonly taken from corpses and put into living people.

Doctors also **transplant** kidneys, livers, and lungs on the operating table.

Surgeons are able to re-attach fingers, arms, or

toes that have been torn or cut off. Modern science even allows burn victims to grow new skin.

Although the human brain has never been transplanted, Dr. Solomon Snyder has grown artificial brain cells.

In some ways, Mary Shelley's novel predicted the future. What seemed fantastic 200 years ago is now common practice in hospitals and medical schools.

Heart transplant

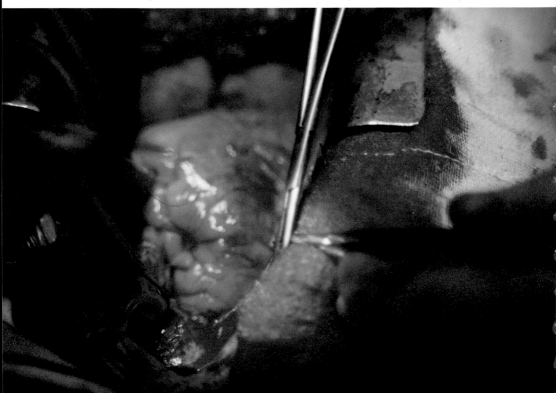

Glossary

abnormal–not able to work normally

classic–one of the best of its kind

decaying–falling apart; rotting

estate–land and money

executed–killed by the government as punishment

fiancée–a woman engaged to marry a man

gallows–platform from which a person is hanged to death

hover–hang in the air, or seem to hang in the air

lurch–walk unevenly; stagger

mourner–person who is sad at the death of another

obsessed with–too interested in, so that a person can think of nothing else

torment–tease with no mercy

transplant–take from one place and put into another; body parts can be taken from one person and put into another

To Learn More

About Frankenstein movies:

Aylesworth, Thomas. *Monsters from the Movies.* Philadelphia: J.B. Lippincott Co., 1972.

Cohen, Daniel. *Masters of Horror.* New York: Clarion Books, 1984.

Green, Carl R., and William R. Sanford. *Bride of Frankenstein.* Mankato, MN: Crestwood House, 1985.

Powers, Tom. *Movie Monsters.* Minneapolis: Lerner Publications, 1989.

_____. *Frankenstein Meets Wolfman.* Mankato, MN: Crestwood House, 1981.

About organ transplants:

Beckelman, Laurie. *The Facts about Transplants.* New York: Crestwood House, 1990.

Facklam, Margery, and Howard Facklam. *Spare Parts for People.* San Diego: Harcourt Brace Jovanovich, 1987.

Lee, Sally. *Donor Banks: Saving Lives with Organ and Tissue Transplants.* New York: Franklin Watts, 1988.

Leinwand, Gerald. *Transplants: Today's Medical Miracles.* New York: Franklin Watts, 1985.

Index

Photo Credits: